About this book

Of course you all know about submarines —
you may have seen one when it has come
into port. But what about all the other
underwater machines? There are tiny
submersibles which are used by one or two
men for exploration or observing
underwater life. Even electric tools can be
used under water, as you can see from the
picture on the cover. There is a lot that we
still have to find out about life under water.
Perhaps in the future the power of the sea
can be harnessed to make electricity, and
underwater machines will be used to make
this dream come true.

MACHINES OF TODAY AND TOMORROW

Farm Machines
Underwater Machines
Space Machines
Fairground Machines
Oil and Machines
Earthmoving Machines

First published in England in 1979 by
Wayland Publishers Limited
49 Lansdowne Place, Hove
East Sussex BN3 1HF, England

Copyright © 1979 Raintree Publishers Inc. and Raintree Publishers
    International Limited

ISBN 0 85340 722 3

Printed in the United States of America

First published in the United States of America by
Raintree Publishers Inc.
under the title **Undersea Machines**

The cover picture shows a diver operating
an underwater drill. (Central Office of
Information.)

Photographs appear through the courtesy of the following
    companies:

Cable and Wireless Development Laboratories: p. 26
D.H.B. Construction Limited: p. 5
General Dynamics, Electric Boat Division: pp. 6 (bottom), 7
Lockheed Missiles and Space Company: pp. 28, 29
Makai Ocean Engineering, photographs by Chuck Peterson: pp. 16,
    17 (bottom)
Royal Navy: pp. 6 (top), 8 (bottom), 9
Tom Stack and Associates, photographs by Ron Church: 11 (bottom),
    14, 15 (top), 23; photographs by Bill Crawford: p.4
U.S. Naval Photographic Center, Naval Station, Washington, D.C.:
    pp. 3, 8 (top), 12, 15 (bottom), 17 (top), 18, 24, 25
U.S. Naval research Laboratory: p.22
Vickers Oceanics: pp. 11 (top), 13, 17
Westinghouse Electric Corporation: p. 23
Woods Hole Oceanographic Institute: pp. 19, 20, 21

Machines of Today and Tomorrow
Underwater Machines
CHRISTOPHER C. PICK

For hundreds of years people have longed to explore under the sea. Today there are many machines that help us to do this. One machine for underwater swimming is called the aqualung. The aqualung holds air in tanks for the diver to breath. This diver is being pulled along by a scuba scooter.

Scuba divers cannot dive very deep. The water would press too hard on their bodies. This diver is wearing a strong diving suit called JIM in which he can go deeper and stay down longer. JIM also carries a lot more air than an aqualung. The big windows make it easy for the diver to see, and the special hands can pick up small objects from the bottom of the sea.

Submarines are big ships which travel under water. They carry enough air, food, and water to stay under the sea for many weeks.

Many submarines are used in war. It is hard to tell the whereabouts of submarines. So they can creep up on ships without warning. They may carry missiles to shoot at targets on land. This submarine carries deadly atomic missiles.

Most submarines carry a large crew. Some crew members spend their time making sure the equipment works. Others do the cooking and look after the rest of the crew's needs.

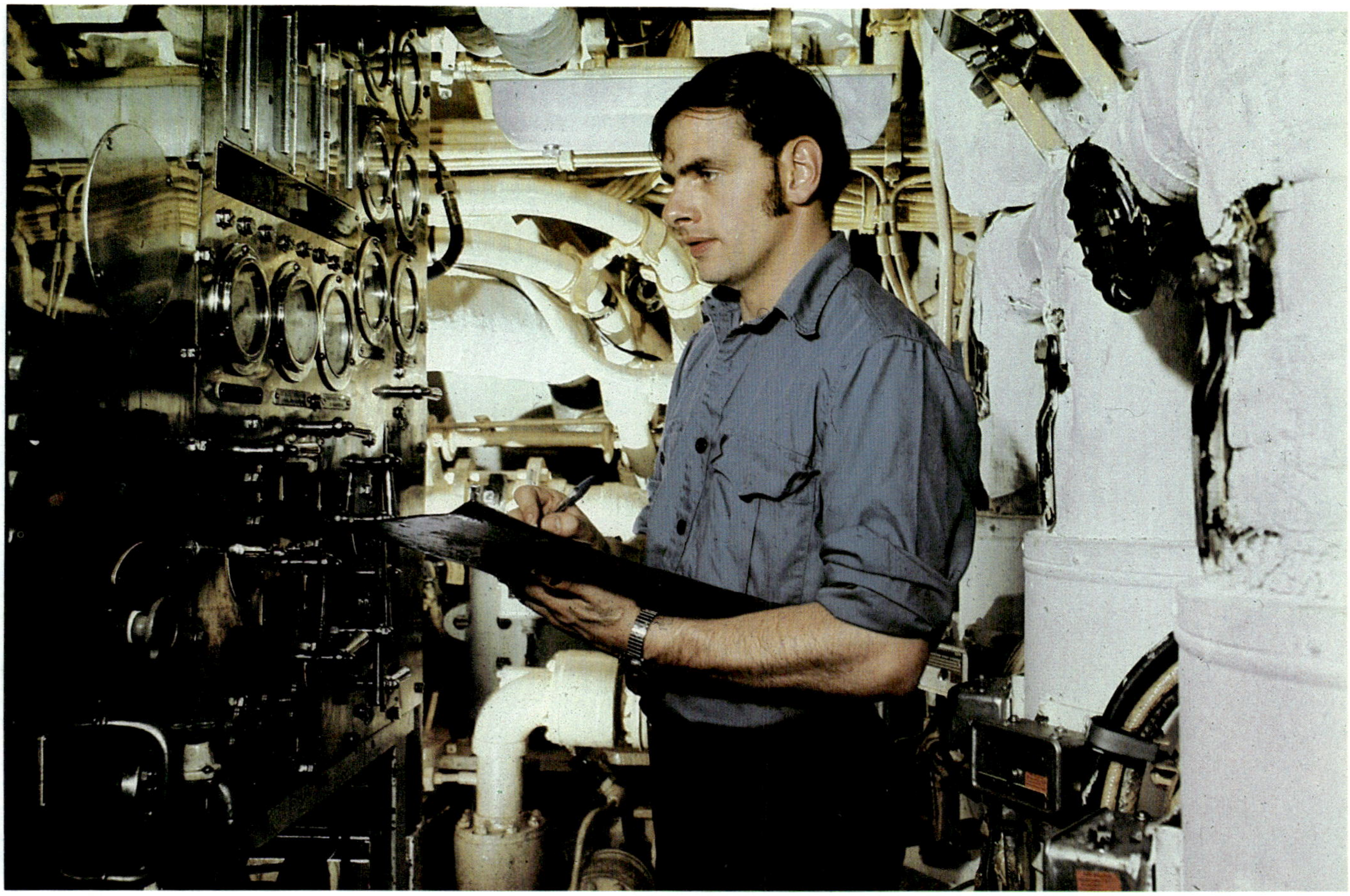

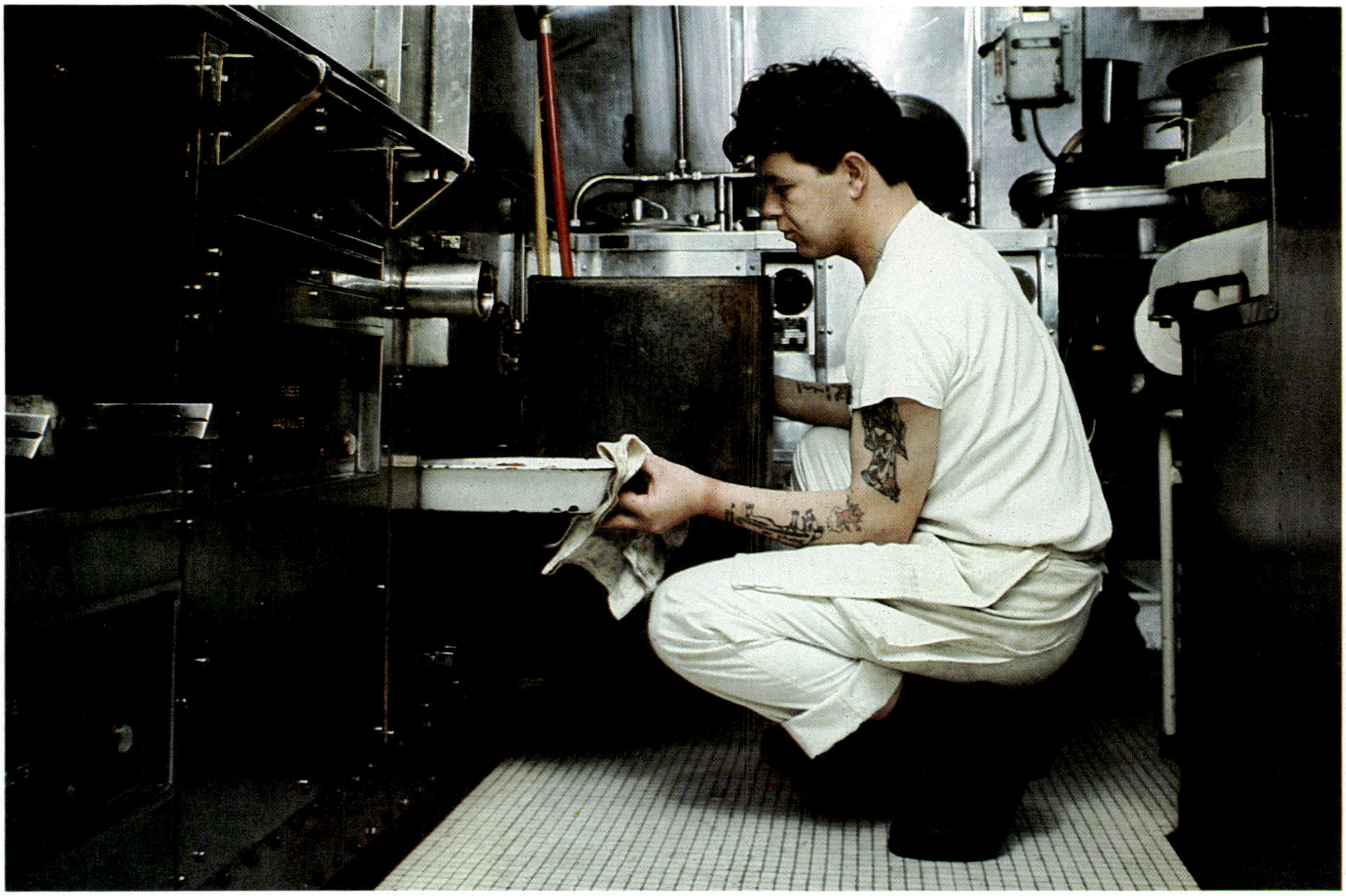

Submersibles are another kind of underwater craft. They are usually much smaller than submarines, and they do not work on their own. Submersibles are carried on a ship which launches them.

Usually, a submersible carries only two or three people. The small space inside is full of equipment to help the crew explore the undersea world. Special arms, cameras, and other equipment are fixed to the outside of the submersible.

This submersible is called NEMO.
It has clear plastic walls. Two
people sit inside and they can watch
underwater building and repair
jobs. NEMO has special electric
plugs so that divers working
outside it can use lights and power
tools.

Divers go out through a special room that is shut off from the rest of the submersible. This room is called a diver lockout system and when they open the door to the sea, water cannot get into the main part.

The most famous underwater
explorer today is a Frenchman
called Jacques Cousteau. One of his
submersibles was called the **Diving
Saucer**. It carried out hundreds of
explorations on the sea-bed to study
underwater plants and animals.

Two **Deepstar** submersibles
were built in the United States with
Cousteau's help. **Deepstar 2000** can
dive to 600 metres under the sea,
and it can stay down for 24 hours.
Deepstar 4000 can go down to
1,200 metres and stay for 8 hours.

For long stays under water, there are submersibles called habitats. People can live and work in them for weeks. Most habitats have double hatches so that divers can go out into the sea to explore.

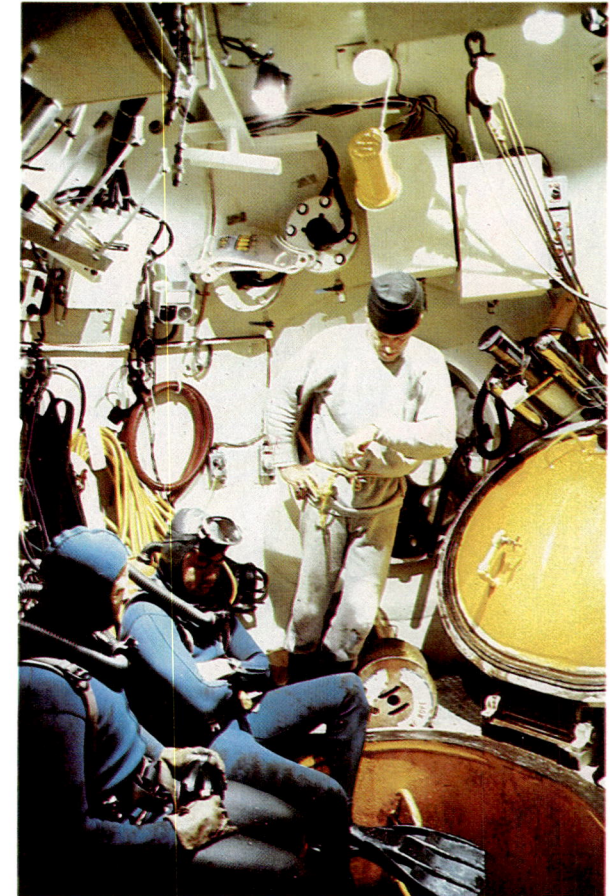

Habitats like these are big enough for four or more people to live and work in comfort.

Some parts of the ocean are too deep for ordinary underwater craft. To explore these very deep places, special craft called bathyscaphes are used. The **Trieste** was one of the first bathyscaphes. It was lowered into the water from a support ship.

In 1960, the **Trieste** set a
record. It went down more than 7
miles (11.3 kilometres) into the
Pacific Ocean. This is a photo of the
floor of the ocean taken from the **Trieste**.

The **Alvin** was the first
deep-diving submarine. It was built
in 1964. It was better than the
Trieste, because it could travel on
its own without a support ship. The
Alvin has made many dives over
1 mile (1.6 kilometres) deep.

This machine is called DOSS. It is used to search for things lost in the ocean. In 1968, the **Alvin** was lost. DOSS found it in about 1 mile (1.6 kilometres) of water.

Another undersea search machine is called OBSS. A ship on the surface pulls it along just above the sea-bed. OBSS was once used to find a hydrogen bomb that was lost in the sea.

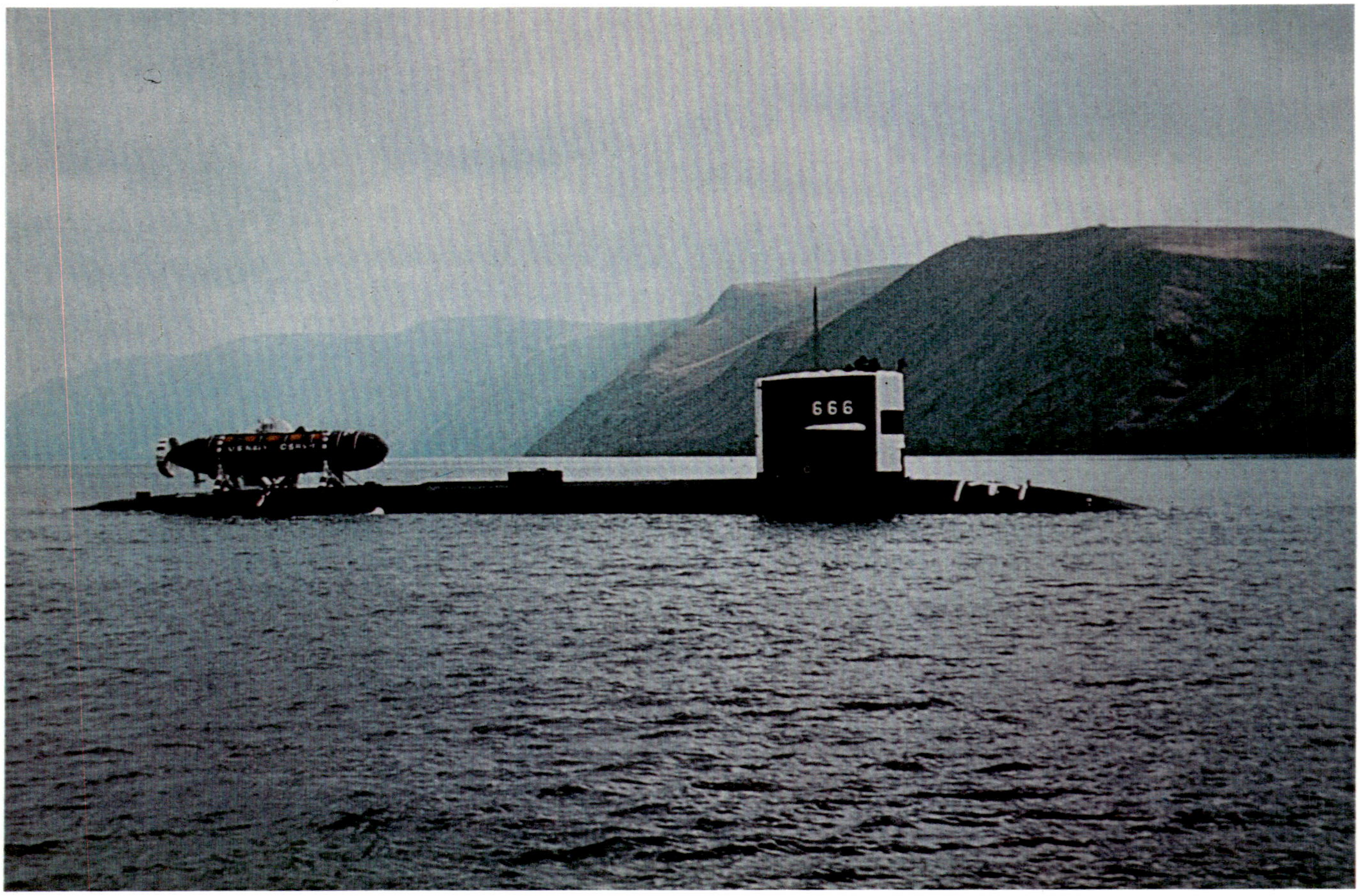
666

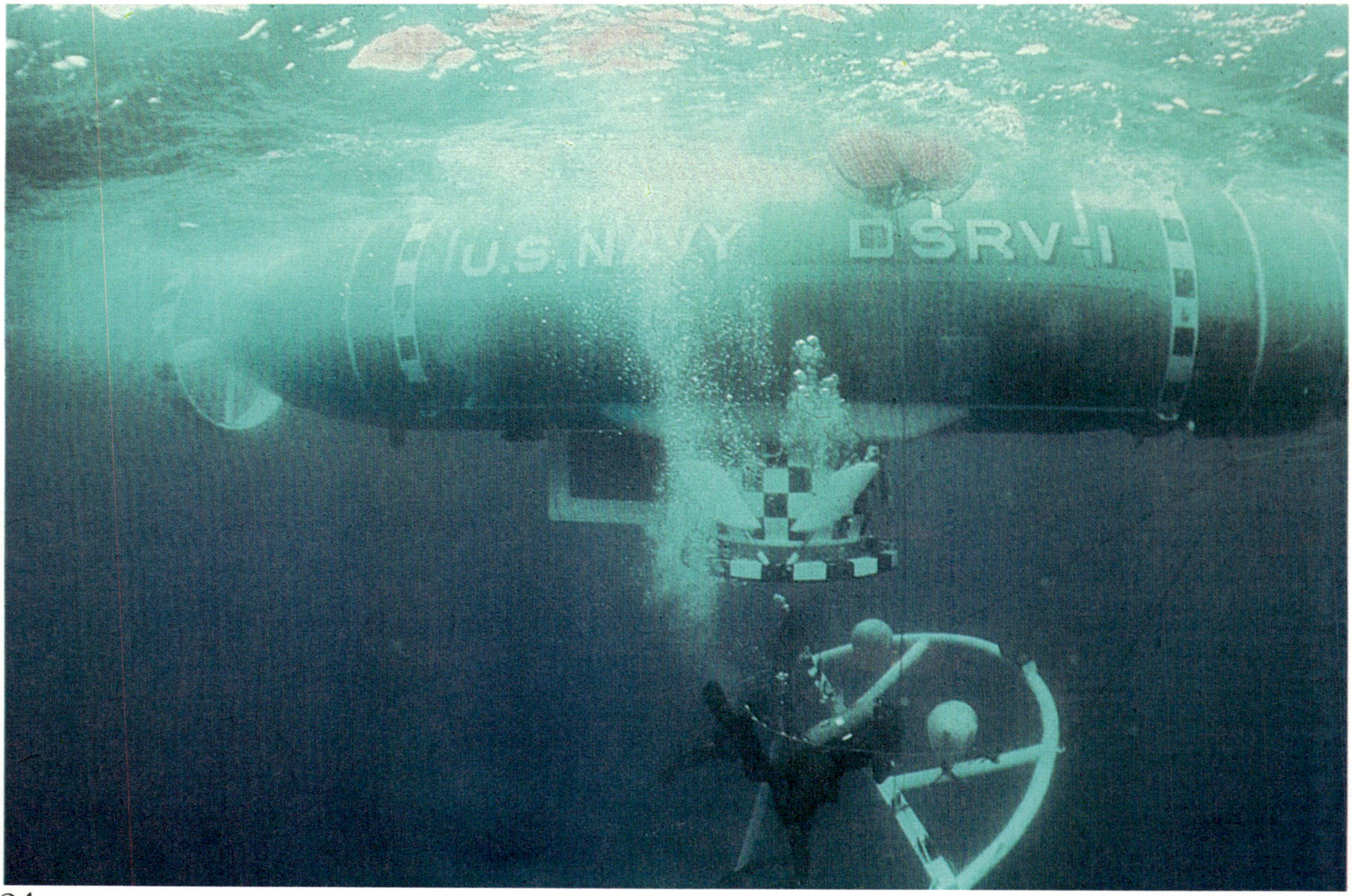
U.S. NAVY
DSRV-1

This is a rescue submersible called a DSRV. It rescues people from submarines that have sunk. The DSRV is carried in an ordinary submarine to the sunken submarine.

The submarine launches the DSRV, which lands on top of the sunken submarine's rescue hatch. The DSRV can carry up to 24 people, and it can go back to the sunken submarine many times.

These telephone cables are laid under the sea so that people in different continents can talk to each other. Many of these cables are laid by a cable ship. The ship can carry up to 900 miles (1,450 kilometres) of cable in special tanks.

The cables lie on the sea-bed and they may be damaged by the water or by things dropped or pulled by ships. This sea-bed crawler, called the **Seacat**, buries the cables in the bottom of the sea with a special tool.

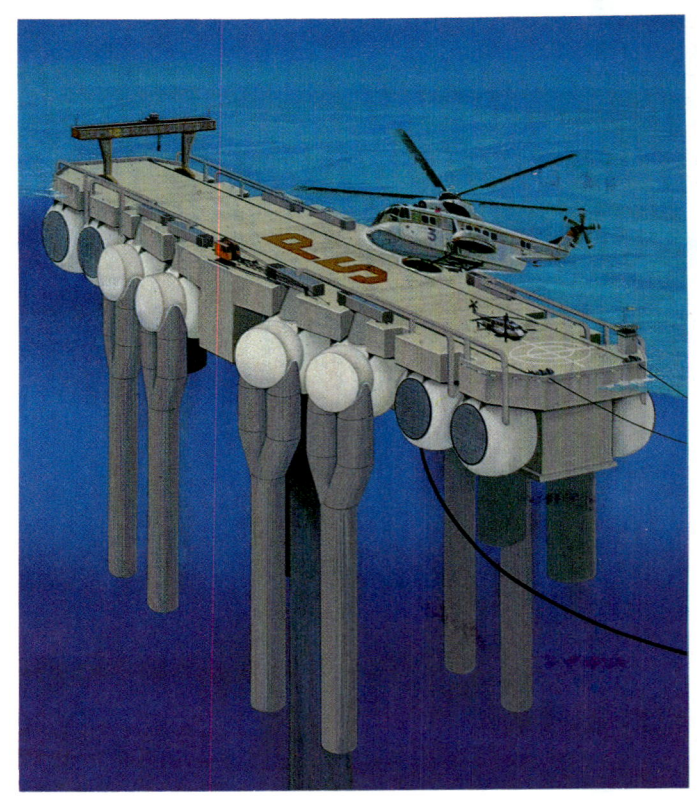

In the future, the oceans may help provide energy. Every day the sun pours down heat which warms up the top layer of the oceans. These machines are designed to change that heat into electricity.

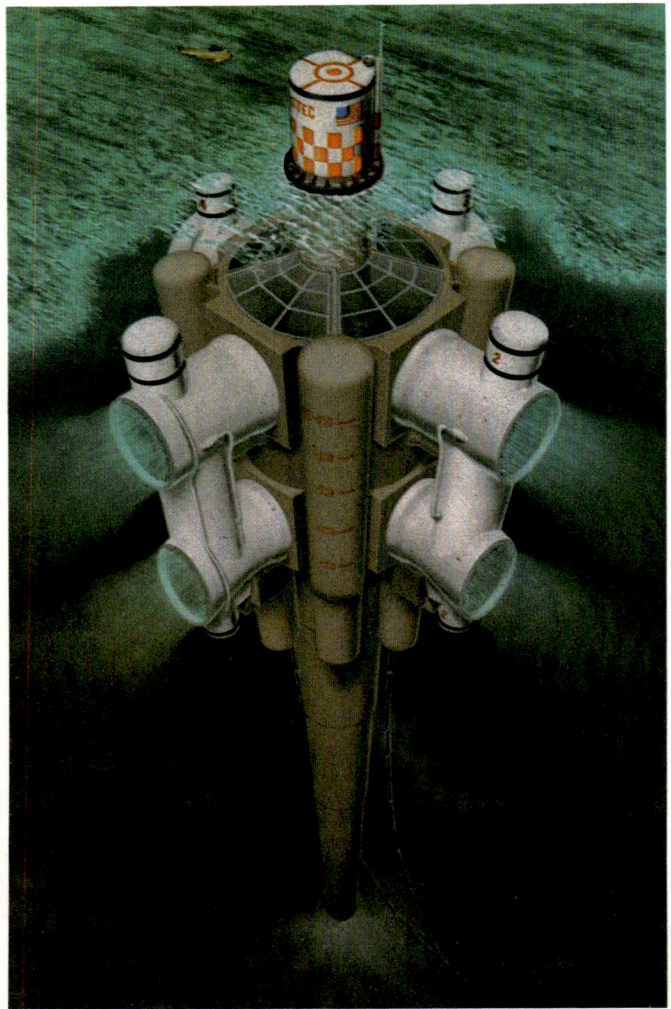

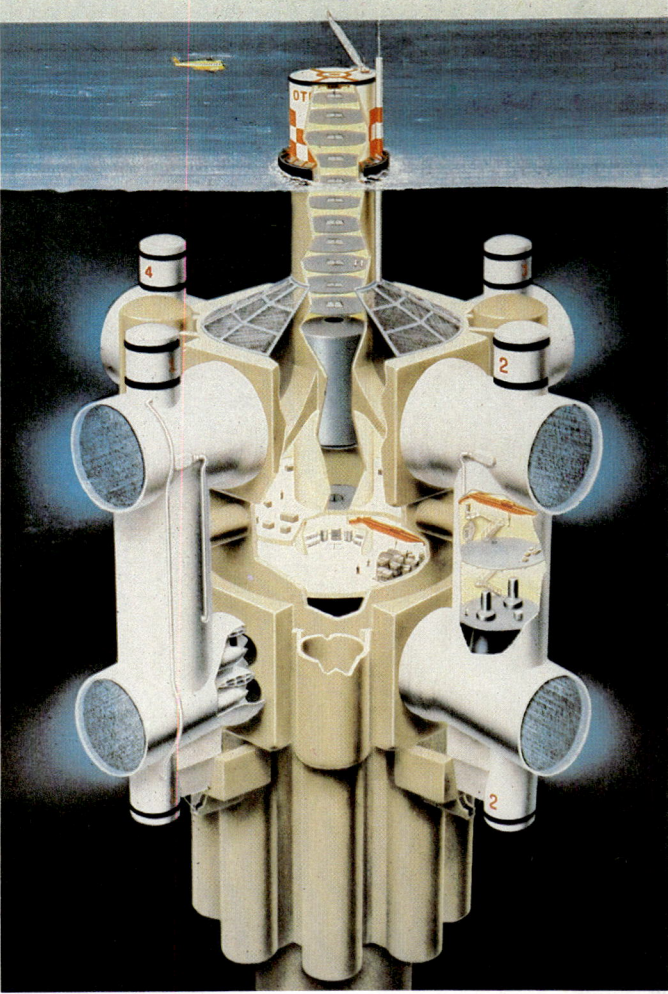

GLOSSARY

aqualung	A lightweight pack which is carried on a diver's back. It holds a lot of air pressed into metal tanks, for the diver to breathe under water.
bathyscaphe	Underwater vessel that is lowered into very deep parts of the ocean.
cable	Telephone wires running along the bottom of the sea; they are specially wrapped so that the water does not damage them.
cable ship	A ship specially built to lay cables on the sea-bed.
cable tank	The space on a cable ship in which the cable is kept until it is ready to be laid.
continent	Large groups of countries, often separated from other groups by seas.
craft	Boat.
crew	The people who work on any kind of ship, submarine or submersible.
DOSS	Deep Ocean Search System; a special undersea tracking machine used to search for objects on the sea-bed.
DSRV	Deep Submergence Rescue Vehicle. A special kind of submersible used to rescue people from a sunken submarine.
diver lockout submersible	A special kind of submersible from which divers can enter the sea outside.
energy	Power provided by fuel.
habitat	A submersible designed for people to remain under the sea for a long time.
hatch	A special kind of door on a submarine or submersible.
launch	To put into the sea, or to fire into the air.
missile	A rocket-shaped weapon which can be fired great distances.
OBSS	Ocean Bottom Scanning Sonar Vehicle. An instrument which explores the shape of the sea-bed and the objects lying on it; it is pulled along above the sea-bed by a ship on the surface of the sea.

ocean	Another word for the sea.
scuba scooter	A machine that can pull a diver along under water.
sea-bed crawler	A machine that crawls along the bottom of the sea.
submarine	A ship that can travel under the sea; modern submarines have a large crew and can stay under the sea for many weeks.
submersible	A craft that travels under the sea; submersibles are much smaller than submarines and can usually only stay under water for a few hours.
support ship	A ship from which a submersible is launched; it stays on the surface of the sea and waits until the submersible returns to it.

INDEX